The Top Six

THREATS

to Civilization

FOOD SHORTAGES

Erin L. McCoy

Cavendish
Square

New York

Library of Congress Cataloging-in-Publication Data

Names: McCoy, Erin L., author.
Title: Food shortages / Erin L. McCoy.
Description: First edition. | New York : Cavendish Square, 2018. |
Series: The top six threats to civilization |
Includes bibliographical references and index.
Identifiers: LCCN 2018023387 (print) | LCCN 2018028274 (ebook) |
ISBN 9781502640673 (ebook) | ISBN 9781502640666 (library bound) |
ISBN 9781502640659 (pbk.)
Subjects: LCSH: Food security–Juvenile literature.
Classification: LCC HD9000.5 (ebook) | LCC HD9000.5 .M368 2018 (print) |
DDC 363.8–dc23
LC record available at https://lccn.loc.gov/2018023387

Editorial Director: David McNamara
Copy Editor: Alex Tessman
Associate Art Director: Alan Sliwinski
Designer: Ginny Kemmerer
Production Coordinator: Karol Szymczuk
Photo Research: J8 Media

Portions of this book originally appeared in *Food Supply Collapse* by Philip Wolny.

The photographs in this book are used by permission and through the courtesy of: Cover Joel Sartore/
National Geographic/Getty Images; pp. 4, 33, 49 Bloomberg/Getty Images; background used throughout
Tflex/Shutterstock.com; background used throughout iulias/Shutterstock.com; 4-5 Trong Nguyen/
Shutterstock.com; p. 7 Stefanie Glinski/AFP/Getty Images; p. 9 Rawpixel.com/Shutterstock.com; p. 10
James Marshall/Corbis Documentary/Getty Images; p. 12 AFP/Getty Images; p. 14 Mohamed Shareef/
Shutterstock.com; p. 16 De Agostini/Biblioteca Ambrosiana/De Agostini Picture Library/Getty Images;
p. 19 Ian Waldie/Getty Images; p. 20 Farooq Naeem/AFP/Getty Images; p. 23 Martin Bureau/AFP/Getty
Images; p. 25 Nicolas Thibaut/Photononstop/Getty Images; p. 28 Belozorova Elena/Shutterstock.com; p.
30 Nigel Cattlin/Alamy Stock Photo; p. 31 Arindambanerjee/Shutterstock.com; p. 35 Hindustan Times/
Getty Images; p. 36 Barcroft Media/Getty Images; p. 38 Raveendran/AFP/Getty Images; p. 40 Dwight Smith/
Shutterstock.com; p. 42 Pierre Vauthey/Sygma/Getty Images; p. 43 AFP/Getty Images; p. 45 Ralph Lee
Hopkins/National Geographic/Getty Images; p. 47 Rawiwano/Shutterstock.com; p. 50 Jeff Greenberg/
Universal Images Group/Getty Images; design elements throughout Iulias/Shutterstock.com

Printed in the United States of America

CONTENTS

Shoppers are running down the supermarket aisles, their baskets full to the brim. You see two people begin to argue over the last jug of water, each tugging on the handle. The checkout lines snake halfway around the store. Holding up the queue, one shopper insists that another share some of the cans in his basket; he's collected every last can of soup in stock. It looks like a fight is about to break out.

In the parking lot, you hear the sound of breaking glass. You turn around and see people rushing into the store, grabbing loaves of bread, bags of rice, and jugs of water. They run out without paying. Store clerks stand outside, dial 911 again and again on their cell phones, but the police never come. When you turn on your car, you hear why: radio news is reporting that there have been break-ins at supermarkets across the city. A few weeks have gone by without any new food to stock area shelves, and people are getting desperate. "I have to feed my family," one person tells the interviewer.

Over the next few nights, food riots break out—and not just in your city. The TV news broadcasts video of fights in front of shuttered

Opposite: A store in Venezuela is shown on August 6, 2015, after having been looted. About 70 percent of consumer products in Venezuela are imported or made from imported materials, so with the value of local currency weakening, importers were unable to pay for goods.

restaurants and grocery stores. A few people show off their bunkers to broadcasters: basements stocked full of canned foods and water. Most people, though, haven't planned ahead in this way. Faucets have run dry, and they spend their days driving longer and longer distances on the hunt for food and water.

THREATS OF HUNGER

Let's stop for a minute and ask ourselves: Is such a crisis really possible?

It depends on whom you ask. A number of factors could lead to a food shortage, and any combination of these could worsen the situation. Many warn that, with the world population increasing more and more quickly, there soon may not be enough food to feed everyone. When large food-producing areas such as California face devastating droughts, the threat of a food or water shortage looms larger. Some fear that our own technologies—such as genetically modified food—could, in an extreme scenario, destroy the world's ability to provide food. And with global warming fundamentally changing climate conditions around the world, crops that once thrived in certain areas may no longer be able to survive there. These and many other factors may cause food shortages that lead to riots, hunger, and widespread panic.

On the other hand, a number of experts have argued that such a future is very unlikely. If we listen to reasonable accounts backed up by science, we can face the future with knowledge rather than panic.

FIGHTING SHORTAGES

An endless amount of food for a growing population is not guaranteed. It takes hard work on the part of scientists and experts across a broad variety of fields to anticipate and prevent food shortages. There are countless farmers, scientists, governments, organizations, and concerned citizens working to ensure future food supplies. The World Bank Group, which provides technical and financial assistance to the developing world and aims to end poverty, has published several issues of the "Food Price Watch," a report monitoring food prices around the globe in the hope of anticipating food shortages and all the problems these can cause. The latest issue reported a 14 percent decrease in food prices worldwide between August 2014 and May 2015 thanks to large stocks of food and improvements in production. This was related to decreased oil prices,

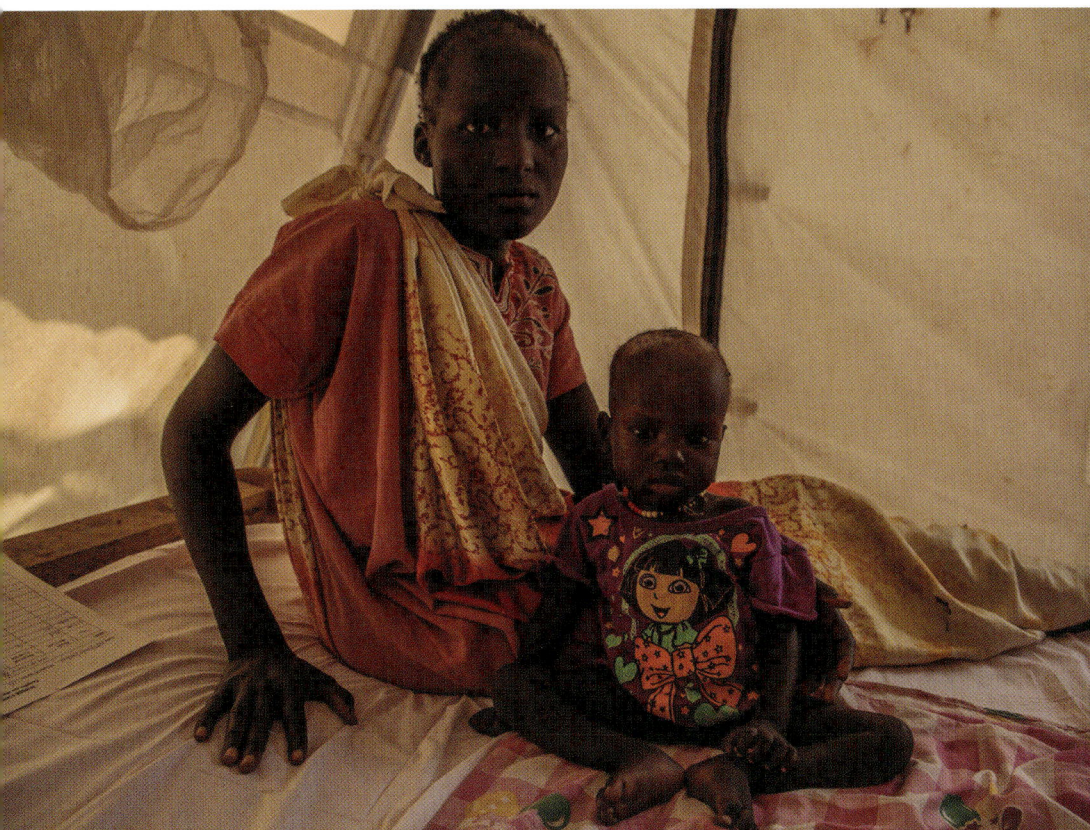

In March 2018, Nyaduol Charlie sits with her one-year-old daughter, who is malnourished because of heavy famine and fighting in South Sudan, where they live.

meaning a decline in the cost of transporting food. Still, according to World Bank senior economist Jose Cuesta, "unexpected domestic food price fluctuations remain a possibility so it is crucial that countries are prepared to address dangerous food price hikes when and if they unfold."

Certainly, the problem is far from solved. A special United Nations (UN) agency, the Food and Agriculture Organization (FAO), is tasked with raising nutrition standards and ensure food supplies. The FAO estimates that 815 million people around the world suffer from chronic hunger. Often, hunger is related more to poverty—and the subsequent inability to buy food—than food shortages. High food prices, though, can exacerbate this, and effectively create shortages in poorer areas of the globe. As the FAO points out, in order to achieve food security—the reliable access to food—we must address questions of diet diversity and access to nutritious food, as well as sanitation and health. The UN's Committee on World Food Security aims to achieve all these ends, focusing on increasing food production while also fighting poverty and investing in health and education. Many other organizations throughout the globe are dedicated to similar ends on international, national, and local levels.

Each nation, business, and individual has a role to play in improving food security. Learning more about all the factors that can contribute to food shortages—and what efforts are being made to mitigate them—can help us determine which worst-case scenarios the world is most and least likely to face in the decades to come.

CHAPTER 1
THE CAUSES OF FOOD SHORTAGE

The journey of food from the farm where it is grown or raised to the table where it is consumed is called a food supply chain or food system. It's a complex, multi-step chain of events, with many potential pitfalls along the way.

For instance, a weather disaster such as drought, or animal and plant diseases or pests, may prevent the food from being grown at all. Transporting food from the place where it is grown to the place where there is a demand for it—sometimes thousands of miles and an ocean away—is challenging not only because food must be kept from spoiling during the journey, but because fluctuating fuel costs can make the journey more expensive. Those costs are often passed on to the person buying the food, but sometimes, they discourage shipment of the food at all. National policies such as tariffs and political situations such as war can determine who has access to food and water, or who can afford to purchase them.

"Food supply" refers to the total amount of food available to the world's population. Most food comes from growing crops, raising livestock, and fishing. Every nation in the world contributes something

Above: The process of first successfully producing food, then transporting it from a farm to someone's table, is quite complex.

to the food supply, however large or small. With so many factors at play, the food supply varies yearly, and from country to country. Some may produce more food than expected one year, others less. A familiarity with the many factors that contribute to food supply can lay the foundation for a deeper understanding of how food shortages happen.

CHALLENGES IN A GLOBAL FOOD SYSTEM

In the distant past, food supplies were local. Towns, regions, and nations raised food locally, trading it or selling it to neighbors. In modern times, technology has changed this drastically. The food supply today is a

Vendors and shoppers crowd into the Oshodi Market in Lagos, Nigeria. Nigeria is the fastest-growing of the top ten largest countries in the world.

complex web of transportation and distribution. Food travels thousands of miles by sea or land between nations and continents. While small farms still produce for local markets, large agricultural companies—together referred to as "agribusiness"—produce food on a scale that would have been unimaginable years ago. Many nations now depend on the international food trade either to drive their economies or to simply provide the food they need. This market has increasingly determined how much all nations pay for basic foods. It also means that a problem affecting one nation's food supply may have global ramifications. Here are some of the many factors that may impact food supply.

A GROWING POPULATION

Perhaps the greatest fear about food comes down to simple mathematics: too many people and too little to eat. The world population is growing more quickly than ever. It hit five billion in 1987, and by 2017 was about 7.6 billion. While opinions vary, the United Nations estimates there will be 9.8 billion people in the world by 2050 and 11.2 billion by 2100.

Much of this growth is expected to happen in developing nations in Asia and Africa, where many people are already undernourished today. Nigeria is the fastest-growing of the world's ten largest countries, and it is expected to be the third most-populous country on Earth by 2050. The forty-seven least-developed countries on the planet tend to have a relatively high fertility rate, at an average of 4.3 births per woman between 2010 and 2015. Faster population growth in poorer countries stands as a primary obstacle to ending hunger and poverty.

Still, fertility around the globe is declining, and in some countries—including China, the United States, and Brazil—the birth rate isn't

As Algeria suffers a drought in 2002, children collect water to drink or sell. Drought not only cuts off essential water supplies; it also threatens to destroy crops, thereby reducing or eliminating essential sources of food.

high enough to maintain the current population. This tends to be the case in more developed countries, and some hope that as more countries develop, this could prevent the global population from reaching unsustainable levels. However, with life expectancy rising, more people are living longer, which in turn increases food demand.

WATER RESOURCES

An adult can survive without food for more than three weeks but can only live without water for about one week. Water comprises at least 60 percent of the human body, so water crises can at times be even more urgent than food crises. Water, though, is a limited resource. About 97 percent of the world's water is in the oceans and is too salty for human consumption. Much of the remaining water is locked in the northern and southern ice caps and in glaciers. The tiny percentage left is what we use for agriculture, drinking, bathing, industry, and other needs.

The way humans use water matters, too. For food-growing regions with little rain, irrigation carries the water to where it is needed to nourish crops, sometimes from far away. Water is drawn from rivers and lakes, and also from groundwater, which collects beneath Earth's surface in soil and rock. In many places, groundwater is being used up faster than it is being replaced.

Agriculture now accounts for as much as 70 percent of the freshwater used by humans, according to the World Bank. Industrial farming, with thousands of acres of crops of thousands of cows or pigs in giant feedlots, uses far more water than the smaller-scale, traditional farms of the past. Some forms of irrigation are much more water-efficient than others, and implementing such practices on a massive scale will be an essential part of assuring future water security.

Between roughly 2014 and when the Earth's population reaches nine billion, agricultural production will have to increase 50 percent, and water usage 15 percent. However, water supplies are now stretched to the breaking point in many regions. As many as four billion people around the globe are already affected by water scarcity, and an estimated five hundred million live in places where the consumption of water is double what is locally renewable. The World Economic Forum has predicted that "water bankruptcy" could occur within the next few decades. One outcome could be a shocking decrease in the production of grains equal to the amount produced today by India and the United States combined.

LAND SHORTAGES

Every year, there is less land available on which to raise food, and Stanford University researchers have predicted that the remaining available arable land may be used up by 2050. Between 35 and 40 percent of the globe's total land area is already being used for agriculture, but not all of it is arable—some terrain is too rugged and difficult to reach, is located in very cold areas, or is characterized by low soil fertility.

Farming and other human activities result in soil erosion and environmental deterioration. In fact, 80 percent of the deforestation occurring across the globe today is as a result of the creation of new pastures for livestock and cropland. Deforestation makes it more likely that fertile soil will wash away, reduces biodiversity by killing off local

Overcrowding in such places as Malé—capital of the Maldives, an island nation—can lead to a scarcity of resources and surging food prices.

animal and plant life, and speeds up global warming by reducing the number of trees available to store greenhouse gases.

In part because of pollution and the degradation of soil, the University of Sheffield's Grantham Centre for Sustainable Futures reported in 2015 that the world had lost almost 33 percent of its arable land in the last forty years. "You think of the dust bowl of the 1930s in North America and then you realise we are moving towards that situation if we don't do something," said Duncan Cameron, a professor of plant and soil biology. Drought, severe erosion, dust storms, and the resultant crop failures in the dust bowl, an area of the United States' high plains region, was one of the contributing factors of the Great Depression.

PESTS AND DISEASE

While the developed world—including the United States, Europe, and Australia—rarely lacks food, poorer nations often have problems feeding their people. Many developed nations have better conditions and land for farming (known as arable land) and use modern, industrial techniques. Poorer nations often have less arable land and access to technology, and because of this may be more likely to suffer crop failures. Extended periods of hunger leading to death and disease, called famines, have occurred throughout history.

However, humans are not the only living creatures that can be affected by disease. In the mid-nineteenth century, Ireland's potatoes were affected by a disease, called "blight," which was a type of fungus, and destroyed potato crops for several years in a row. Potatoes had supplied as much as 60 percent of Ireland's food needs. However, as in so many cases of food shortage and famine, the blight was not the only cause of the widespread hunger that eventually killed about one million

An 1847 illustration depicts the hunger and suffering that prevailed during the Irish potato famine.

Irish people. At the time, predominantly Catholic Ireland was controlled by Protestant England. Each side held deep prejudices toward the other, and many Protestants believed that the famine represented a kind of divine judgment against Catholics. What's more, a laissez-faire policy on the part of the British held that government should interfere as little as possible in the economy, so the starving Irish received little aid. In the end, political response to the blight was just as responsible for the famine as the blight itself was.

Plant pests and diseases can cause significant crop losses and destroy pastures upon which livestock rely for sustenance. They can be spread by insects, through the trade of products, or by wind and weather. They are a primary threat to food security, according to the FAO, which lists locusts, fruit flies, armyworms, wheat rust, and cassava and banana diseases "among the most destructive transboundary plant pests and diseases."

Breeding Higher-Yield Crops

In the 1950s and 1960s, people worried that the exploding population in the developing world would soon lead to famine. Scientists worked to breed crops that produced higher yields, or harvests. Norman Borlaug, an agricultural scientist, helped develop high-yield wheat to grow in tropical regions. It was later used in India, Pakistan, and other countries.

Synthetic, or artificial, fertilizers and huge irrigation projects were also introduced. Farmers were able to produce much more food on the same amount of land. According to *U.S. News & World Report*, new strains, or varieties, of wheat and rice led to a 21 percent increase in crop yields in the developing world from 1961 to 1980. From 1981 to 2000, they rose by 50 percent.

Some called the combined use of these technologies the "Green Revolution." For his work, Borlaug received the Nobel Peace Prize in 1970.

WEATHER, GLOBAL WARMING, AND DROUGHT

A stable and growing food supply also depends on favorable weather. Drought, or too little rain, can severely disrupt crops. Too much rain—either from floods or from natural disasters like tsunamis—can also be disastrous. Many crops only grow under certain conditions. Extreme weather, such as a heat wave or a late frost, can reduce or wipe out harvests.

Another great concern is global warming, which is a rise in average worldwide temperatures that the vast majority of scientists agree is largely caused by human activity, such as emissions from factories and automobiles. Global warming is blamed for complex changes in weather patterns around the world. Some regions face hotter, drier summers than ever before, while others experience greater flooding. Conditions for growing food could become more unpredictable and extreme in the coming years.

Global warming is also affecting our water supply in previously unimaginable ways. Glaciers in the Tibetan Plateau could melt partly or entirely in the coming century. As leading water expert Dr. Peter Gleick has told the *Nation*, "Just about every major Asian river originates in the Tibetan Plateau." Up to one billion people in China, India, and other nations depend on these rivers for drinking and irrigation water.

Whether or not global warming is to blame, the so-called Millennium Drought in Australia between 2001 and 2009 severely affected wheat production, causing billions of dollars in losses and affecting wheat prices. It was described by researchers looking back on it in 2013 as "the worst drought on record for southeast Australia." The US state of California has also suffered severe droughts, triggering the declaration of a state of emergency in 2014 that was not lifted until three years

Gordon Litchfield, a livestock farmer, surveys a completely dry dam on his property in Leigh Creek, Australia, at the height of a drought in 2005.

later. California produces more than one-third of the vegetables and two-thirds of the fruits and nuts consumed in the United States.

AN INTERNATIONAL FOOD CRISIS

Several events overlapped starting in 2007, and a global food crisis made headlines around the world. Droughts were already plaguing Australia and southern Africa, and poor weather had affected crop yields in China, Europe, and elsewhere.

Other recent trends caused lower output in important grains. The United States exported less because many farmers no longer grow grains for food. Instead, they receive subsidies, or government payments, for raising certain crops to make "biofuels." Biofuels are crop-based alternatives to gasoline, such as ethanol, that are made from corn.

Important grain-producing nations such as India and Kazakhstan limited exports to guarantee food for their own people. High oil prices also greatly increased costs for farming, trucking, and shipping. World prices for rice, wheat, corn, meat, and other foods skyrocketed.

The changing appetites of nations also affected prices. In India and especially China, expanding economies meant that millions of people were entering the middle class. Their new wealth led them to adopt more Western-style diets. As food expert Harriet Friedmann told the Canadian Broadcasting Corporation (CBC), "Meat is the new norm, even in countries like India, which used to be almost entirely vegetarian." However, raising livestock for meat takes an estimated four times as

During an international food crisis in 2008, Pakistani women line up to collect rice at the Bari Imam Shrine in Islamabad in April 2008.

much grain than using grain directly as food. Consequently, more people eating meat meant less grain on the world market, which drove up prices.

Weather, economics, and human habits had combined to create a "perfect storm" for a food supply crisis. When prices soared, it was the poorest who suffered most. Anger and desperation soon exploded into violence. Rioters emptied supermarkets in Harare, Zimbabwe's capital, while at least twenty-four people died in riots in Cameroon, as people rebelled against the high cost of fuel and food. Unrest spread in other African nations such as Burkina Faso, Senegal, the Ivory Coast, and Mauritania. Protests also broke out in Mexico, Pakistan, Bangladesh, and Uzbekistan. Protestors in Haiti chanting "We're hungry!" eventually forced the resignation of the prime minister. In Egypt, the government ordered soldiers to bake bread for civilians. The issue of food had suddenly become a security issue, and headlines around the world predicted more trouble to come.

FOOD RIOTS

What is a food riot? There is no easy consensus on this issue. Nonetheless, the World Bank defines two types of food riot: type 1 riots are motivated by food-price inflation and often involve protests directed against the government, whose policies or subsidy programs may have left citizens dissatisfied or upset. Type 2 riots are caused by extreme food shortages and are generally less politically motivated and therefore less likely to direct animosity at a government entity. Rather, they target food supplies, meaning people might raid or attack grocery stores or food-shipment facilities and transportation, such as trucks. The latter type generally results in fewer casualties, because fewer people tend to be involved and because they are usually less organized.

The five most deadly type 1 riots between 2007 and 2014 occurred in Africa and the Middle East, with the deadliest being the one in Cameroon. Thirty-seven people died in South Africa in August 2012 after a swift increase in the price of food. Tunisia, Yemen, and Mozambique also saw fatalities. In some cases, protestors were shot by police who were attempting to control the riots.

The deadliest type 2 riots between 2007 and 2014 were more widespread, occurring everywhere from China to Pakistan. Twenty-two people died in Argentina in December 2012, when teenagers in the province of Buenos Aires began to ransack grocery stores; more than two hundred people around the nation were injured, and President Fernando de la Rua resigned. In Pakistan, at least twenty people were trampled in riots in 2009. Somalia saw two deadly riots in 2007 and 2011; in both cases, people were attempting to raid trucks or warehouses containing food. In 2007, three people in China were trampled as many ran to grab bottles of cooking oil, whose price had skyrocketed.

More recently, in January 2018, hundreds of Venezuelans looted a supermarket, a truck loaded with corn, and a food collection center in the state of Merida after four years of economic recession had left millions of citizens in poverty. Mobs reportedly slaughtered cattle. At least four people died.

FOOD AND THE ARAB SPRING

Food riots are believed by some to have been a key factor in sparking what became known as the Arab Spring. Riots broke out in at least fourteen North African and Middle Eastern countries. Countries such as Egypt rely almost entirely on imports from other nations to supply the grains necessary for making bread. The fact that much of the population relies on government-funded subsidies—or financial assistance—to keep the cost of bread low also makes populations especially reliant on their governments, according to *Boston Globe* correspondent and Century Foundation fellow Thanassis Cambanis. It also means they are more upset at their governments when prices spike, as they did in 2008.

By 2010 and 2011, protests were popping up throughout North Africa and the Middle East. Tunisian protesters waved baguettes, while Egyptians chanted, "Bread, freedom, social justice." Protestors toppled their heads of state or mounted significant uprisings in Tunisia, Egypt, Yemen, Bahrain, and Syria. In Syria, where the conflict was ongoing

A Tunisian protestor displays a baguette during an Arab Spring protest on January 18, 2011.

in 2018, the regime has systematically blocked rebels' access to food, using famine as a weapon.

These events, the World Bank reports, "have underscored the close relationship between food insecurity and conflict, a relationship that until recently was mostly associated with the food-related humanitarian disasters and famines recurrently observed in the course of civil and intrastate wars." Meanwhile, the food price increases that helped to spark the Arab Spring have drawn attention to the relationship between food-related conflicts and political instability.

CHAPTER 2
A FOOD-SUPPLY COLLAPSE

Speculation abounds on how a future food shortage—or, in the worst-case scenario, a complete food-supply collapse—could take place. Land, water, or food supplies could run out, or a disaster such as drought or disease might destroy huge swaths of crops. High fuel prices might leave fruit rotting on the vine. Global warming might fundamentally change climate patterns and leave key agricultural areas unable to produce. Was the food crisis of 2008 just the tip of the iceberg?

Droughts, disease, and war have affected food supplies since the dawn of civilization. Even though the twentieth century ushered in better technology and farming techniques, we have not been able to prevent famines or eliminate hunger. The weather is mostly beyond our control—although the choices we make that alleviate or exacerbate global warming will affect long-term climate change and weather patterns. How we use land, water, and other resources may have more immediately visible effects on future food security. We have taken for granted that we could always count on these resources. What would happen if they started running out?

Above: A 1989 war between Mauritania and Senegal was waged over access to the waters of the River Senegal, shown here.

Seas—and Seafood— in Peril

In 2008, an international panel warned that greenhouse gases are endangering the world's oceans, which have absorbed carbon dioxide and grown more acidic. "The chemistry is so fundamental and changes so rapid and severe that impacts on organisms appear unavoidable," Dr. James Orr, a chemical oceanographer, told the *New York Times*. The panel said that coral reefs, shellfish, and other sea life had been affected, and that the problem threatens all sea life.

Overfishing is also endangering our oceans' food supplies. Small fish that the entire marine food chain depends on are at particular risk, marine biologist Margot Stiles told the *San Francisco Chronicle*: "They're the foundation of the food web. Without them, we would lose the things we really care about—the seabirds, whales, tuna, and salmon."

WATER WARS

In 2006, London newspaper the *Independent* reported that British military planners were making long-term preparations for "disaster relief, peacekeeping, and warfare" in anticipation of conflicts down the line over water and other resources. Likewise, then–US secretary of state Hillary Clinton said in 2012 that water scarcity raises "serious national security concerns." As populations grow, more people will need water for drinking, bathing, manufacturing, farming, and other uses. Many cultures—especially in the developed world—take water for granted. Much of it is wasted, or is made unusable through pollution. Skipping ahead to the year 2030, we can imagine a world where the struggle for resources leads to conflict—even war.

This may be happening already. Some analysts have indicated that Israel's war against Arab armies in 1967, and its continued occupation of the Golan Heights region, may be related to its need to control water supplies. A 1989 war between Mauritania and Senegal was fought over access to grazing areas beside the River Senegal. And other experts say that water scarcity helped spark the ongoing civil war in Syria.

In a world where one might imagine water wars breaking out, billions lack access to clean water. Too much irrigation has reduced once-mighty rivers to streams, and groundwater supplies are nearly exhausted. Climate change has transformed fertile plains into deserts and wiped out glaciers. Crop yields decrease. Many nations deplete their food reserves or accuse their neighbors of taking too much water from sources that are drying out. Prices for rice and wheat surpass those of gold or silver. Water is rationed. Warships must escort tankers full of food and water across the oceans for fear of attack.

Machines used in agriculture burn a great deal of fuel and emit greenhouse gases, contributing to the energy crisis.

Governments, accused by their people of hoarding food, are overthrown, and entire regions are battered by civil war. Nations fight over the precious regions where food can still be raised. Food-producing areas become battlefields, resulting in more scarcity. Some leaders threaten the use of nuclear weapons.

FOOD AND THE ENERGY CRISIS

We take the food we buy for granted, rarely thinking about how it was produced or transported to us. Modern agriculture depends on petroleum, or oil, in many ways. Farm equipment and vehicles such as tractors run on petroleum-derived fuels. These machines are used to plant seeds in the ground and to harvest crops. Fuel is needed to transport livestock and crops. Imagine the amount of oil used by the trucks, trains, and ships that transport food around the world every day.

Much of the fertilizer used in modern farming is made with petrochemicals, products made from natural gas or oil. Their widespread use has made it possible to produce large amounts of food inexpensively. Food is also cheaper in recent years than ever before partly because of the ready availability of these fuels. However, the hidden costs of inexpensive energy may come back to haunt us in the coming years.

That's because many people predict that, much like water and land, oil and other fuels are running out. Unless large new deposits are discovered, experts believe that the remaining oil in the world could start to run out by the middle of the twenty-first century.

A drastic decrease in oil or gas supplies would make farming many more times expensive than it is now. Gigantic yields from places like the midwestern United States would become a thing of the past. Food production worldwide would drop, even as the population reached record levels. Dozens of nations that import much of their food would see transportation prices climb even higher. The price of producing food and getting it to where it is needed would skyrocket, putting millions of people at risk of hunger. These are just the problems that we would face if oil supplies were limited, but still available. The end of oil could spell doom for modern agriculture, bringing it to a grinding halt.

DISEASE AND CROP FAILURE

Plants also suffer from diseases, and plagues have caused crop failures for thousands of years. One frightening scenario arose in early 2007, with the appearance of Ug99, a strain of black stem rust fungus, which destroys wheat. Although most wheat grown since the 1960s is resistant to most strains, it is vulnerable to Ug99. Starting in East Africa, spores of the fungus have spread through the Middle East, and new strains

Ug99 is a strain of fungus that destroys wheat, endangering crops and threatening to cause food shortages.

have appeared in Europe. Could a wheat disease, or another as-yet-undiscovered disease, wipe out crops on entire continents?

In late 2017, there were reports that a protein had been identified that sparks a wheat gene resistant to Ug99. Researchers had been studying ways to fight back against the fungus for several years. The breakthrough would help with the breeding of Ug99-resistant wheat. Nevertheless, this does not mean that future crop diseases might not cause more dramatic crop failures, spread more quickly, or prove more difficult to battle.

GENETICALLY MODIFIED FOODS

In recent decades, scientists have used genetic engineering and other forms of biotechnology to create new versions of crops and even animals. These include everything from wheat that is super-resistant to insects to bigger, juicier tomatoes and extra-nutritious rice with crop yields five times larger than other strains. Varieties of corn and other crops have been created that need less water and are resistant to diseases. Many genetically modified (GM) foods have created incredible crop yields around the world. With a possible worldwide food crisis approaching, some believe that biotechnology will be the key to a new Green Revolution. But could there be a dark side to genetically modified organisms (GMOs)?

Some critics of GM foods call them "Frankenfoods." They argue that tampering with genes can be harmful, even deadly, for humans or livestock, and campaign for the widespread labeling of food containing GMOs. Some improved GMOs use genes from other species—for

During a demonstration against GMO-seed producer Monsanto in May 2013, protestors speak out for clearer labeling of foods containing GMOs.

example, proteins from animals or even bacteria. Opponents of GM foods claim that introducing new genes that have never been part of the food supply is particularly risky.

Imagine a gene added to corn and wheat, for example, that greatly improves the speed at which they grow. These miracle crops are planted all over the world, feeding billions. A little-known side effect of the gene, however, is that it creates deadly poisons in the human body after a few years. Or perhaps it takes a few harvests before the gene mutates, creating corn and wheat to which humans are allergic.

After many mysterious deaths, humanity realizes it must destroy 90 percent of the world's supply of these grains. The poisonous wheat and corn have been used to make many products—breakfast cereals, cooking oils, livestock feed, and hundreds of others—all of which must be destroyed. Imagine the panic as whole supermarkets are emptied of these contaminated products, with little left to replace them.

Critics also fear that GMOs are susceptible to "genetic pollution," or "gene flow." GMOs could cross-breed with non-GMOs, and genes added to crops could jump to other plants in unpredictable ways. Certain GM crops contain genes developed to resist herbicides, the chemicals that farmers use to eliminate weeds. Some believe that such genes could potentially spread to weeds themselves, creating "superweeds" that herbicides could no longer control. Superweeds could spread quickly, destroying millions of acres of farmland.

More realistic concerns around GMOs relate to their accessibility to smaller and poorer farm operations. For example, huge companies such as Monsanto have patented their genetically modified seeds and require farmers to buy the seeds again and again every year, rather than replanting seeds from the previous year's crop. Such companies have become so powerful that just three—Monsanto, DuPont, and Syngenta—control 53 percent of the global seed market. More than 90 percent of US soybeans are grown from such seeds.

However, just a few companies having such immense control over food supplies has some people concerned. They worry that the world's poorest farmers and other small operations that want to stay competitive by selling these higher-yield crops may not be able to afford the seeds. Monsanto has sued hundreds of farmers for patent infringement because they replanted seeds. "Corporations did not create seeds and many are challenging the existing patent system that allows private companies to assert ownership over a resource that is vital to survival and that

A worker weighs hybrid cucumber seeds at a Monsanto division in the Netherlands in 2016.

historically has been in the public domain," Debbie Barker, an expert with Save Our Seeds, told the *Guardian* newspaper in 2013.

Many also worry that, because GMOs of a single crop variety can be very genetically similar, there is not enough genetic diversity among them. Where there is diversity, some crops or individual plants might prove more resistant to disease than others. Without this genetic diversity, the right disease could wipe out a huge percentage of the world's genetically modified crops, all at once.

CHAPTER 3

DEBUNKING WORST-CASE SCENARIOS

Predictions regarding the future of food security can be frightening, or even make the situation feel hopeless. Each of the worst-case scenarios described in Chapter 2 have some basis in fact. However, many experts argue that such extreme cases are unlikely, and many others are actively working to prevent them from ever occurring.

FACTORS CREATING HUNGER

In the modern era, many food crises occurred not from lack of food but because of other factors. Wars and political problems have been major causes of famine and other food shortages. Prices on world food markets, meanwhile, are inevitably subject to change depending on how much farmers around the world plant and harvest in any given year. Some years, a surplus will drive down the price of wheat, and farmers will plant less as a result. The following year's wheat yield might be much lower.

Of all the causes of the food crises of 2007 and 2008, a global lack of food was not one of them. As Josette Sheeran, the World Food Programme's executive director, told the *Guardian*, "This is the new face

Above: On July 30, 2017, people protest the skyrocketing price of tomatoes in New Delhi, India.

of hunger … There is food on shelves, but people are priced out of the market." There are many ways that the world can act now to reduce hunger and guarantee the world's food in the future. Once we recognize this, we come to realize that food-supply collapse is far from inevitable.

MAKING FOOD GO FARTHER

We cannot continue to take our land and water resources for granted. However, a world in which nations are fighting for the last drops of water or plots of land is only a remote possibility. We can avoid this fate by making better use of our resources. By becoming more efficient, eliminating waste, and changing our habits, we can do more with less.

Self-styled "freegans" are people who collect food that has been thrown away by restaurants and grocery stores to save money and reduce waste.

Roughly 40 percent of all the food grown in the world is never eaten by anyone; rather, it is actually thrown away, says Jonathan Foley, California Academy of Sciences executive director. In developing countries, 40 percent of this waste occurs after harvest and during the processing of food. In the industrialized world, 40 percent occurs at the retail or consumer stages. In the European Union

(EU), there is now a movement to reduce food waste. The European Commission's website outlines several causes of food waste, including misunderstandings about what the "use by" and "best before" dates on food really mean. One of the EU's Sustainable Development Goals is to cut retail- and consumer-level food waste in half by 2030. Ugly fruit markets, which sell vegetables and fruits once thrown away simply because they weren't aesthetically pleasing, are popping up around the EU and in the United States.

Eating less meat is another potential solution. An estimated 75 percent of agricultural land is used to grow food for livestock, which we later eat. In 2016, China's health ministry released recommendations that would reduce meat consumption in the country by 50 percent, according to the *Guardian*. If these guidelines are followed, the Chinese livestock industry could decrease its carbon dioxide–equivalent emissions by 56 percent by the year 2030. This would be a huge step forward from the world's most populous nation, considering that 14.5 percent of emissions that cause global warming are produced by the livestock industry. That's more emissions than the entire global transportation sector emits. And with less land dedicated to producing feed for livestock, the initiative—and others like it—could potentially result in the production of more crops for human consumption.

RESPONSIBLE WATER USE

As Dr. Peter Gleick explains in an interview with the *Nation*, "Water is a renewable resource, mostly. After it is used, it just goes somewhere else in the hydrologic [water] cycle, and it comes back. And so we are not literally running out of water." He adds, however, that "much of our water depends on unsustainable groundwater use." Therefore, governments, cities, towns, farmers, and individuals must commit to more responsible freshwater usage to ensure that groundwater and other reservoirs have sufficient time to be replenished.

One reason people waste water is because, in much of the developed world, it is so cheap and seems so available. In 2006, the *Independent* reported that citizens of certain African nations—for example, Gambia and Mozambique—use less than 10 liters (2.6 gallons) per person daily, while the average US citizen uses about 500 liters (132 gallons).

Scientific American has outlined some ideas for water conservation. One idea is to raise prices on water use. Cities would be forced to improve their water systems to cut waste, and citizens would be less likely to use so much of this more expensive resource. With extra money from water sales, cities could also afford to improve their systems, preventing leakage and breakdowns that can lead to further waste.

Many farms around the world use inefficient irrigation methods. Saving just 10 percent more a year could free up vast quantities. One

Children in New Delhi, India, commemorate World Earth Day with a rally. They also collected the signatures of more than 100,000 students pledging to save water.

way is to line leaky irrigation channels with waterproof materials. Another is to take advantage of the seasons. Much water is wasted because snowmelt and rain runoff often occur during the nongrowing season. The use of underground water storage tanks, which experience less evaporation than water held behind dams in reservoirs, could conserve such runoff for drier growing seasons. Also, more farms could employ drip-irrigation systems, which insert water into the soil where crops need it, rather than spraying it up into the air, which leads to more evaporation.

We learned in Chapter One that raising livestock like cows and pigs takes many times more grain than using grain simply as food. The same is true for water. The World Water Council estimates that raising 1 pound (0.5 kilograms) of beef takes thirteen times as much water as growing 1 pound (0.5 kg) of wheat. Encouraging diets with more vegetables and less meat would go a long way toward reducing water use.

Farmers could also concentrate on cultivating crops that are less water-intensive, at least in drier areas. Potatoes need the least water, while rice needs the most. New varieties of crops could be developed—either with biotechnology or natural breeding—that use less water. If consumers are educated to make the right choices, we could all contribute with our "water-friendly" diets.

Finally, we could harness another important source of water: the world's oceans. Desalinization plants pump seawater and remove the salt, making the water drinkable and usable for agriculture. The greatest number of these facilities exist in Middle Eastern countries such as Saudi Arabia, where freshwater is scarce. Desalinization is uncommon because it has been traditionally very expensive. However, scientists are working on new technologies to desalt water more cheaply and using less energy.

The use of renewable energy technologies—such as these solar photovoltaic collectors, set up in a California vineyard—can reduce the environmental impact of food production.

THE NEXT GREEN REVOLUTION

We cannot count on fossil fuels such as oil to last forever. Rather than panic, the challenge is to limit our dependence on them. Doing so will help us fight global warming and bring on a new age of agriculture—perhaps even the next Green Revolution.

Using energy wisely means cutting down on fossil fuels. Fertilizers not made from oil or natural gas could be an option. More efficient farming techniques would reduce the need for fossil fuels. Many people have already started buying more locally grown—even urban-grown—foods, reducing the need to transport food long distances.

Using less fossil fuel for other purposes—such as driving, heating our homes, and industry—also means freeing up more for our food needs. Biofuels are a possible solution, though they remain controversial because they redirect grains out of the food supply. Better mileage for motor vehicles, retrofitting homes to be energy-efficient, and other measures would help the food supply and the environment. Alternative energies, too, could also help power a new generation of agriculture. These may include such renewable energy sources as wind, hydroelectric, and solar power.

A Doomsday Prophet

People have predicted the end of the food supply for centuries. In 1798, Englishman Thomas Malthus became famous for his book, *An Essay on the Principle of Population.* He predicted that human populations would always grow faster than their food supplies could feed them.

Malthus was wrong, however. England experienced a technological revolution in the years after his essay, with new seeds, machines, and fertilizers helping to increase food production. Population growth has also been slower than he expected: as standards of living have increased, family size has decreased.

Similar forecasts were made in the middle of the twentieth century, and the Green Revolution proved these wrong as well. However, the twenty-first century brings new challenges. Malthus's predictions serve as a reminder that previous generations have met the challenge of food supply in innovative ways.

DEBUNKING THE GMO THREAT

Genetically modified foods have been controversial for years. Obviously, any new technology needs rigorous safety testing. However, most credible scientists insist there is little proof that GM foods could harm humans or our food supply.

In an interview with *Newsweek*, biologist Robert Zeigler, then-director of the International Rice Research Institute (IRRI), said, "People will see over the coming years that molecular tools and genetic engineering are not inherently dangerous. We have been growing GM crops for well over a decade now in North America on vast acreages, and no harm has been done to anything or anybody." While the IRRI recognizes that there are concerns over the development of GM foods, it supports the careful development of GMOs within biosafety regulations. US government agencies have also declared it safe for public consumption.

The threat of genetic pollution, or gene flow, may also be overblown. Some instances have indeed been documented, as in a case in which genetically engineered grass on golf courses hybridized with wild creeping bentgrass. Still, as Heather Landry, then a Ph.D. candidate in Harvard University's Biological and Biomedical Sciences Program, wrote, "it is important to recognize that cross-pollination is not equally likely for all crops. Many crops commonly cultivated in the US, such as corn, soybeans, and cotton, are not perennials and do not have wild relatives growing in close proximity."

CHAPTER 4

GLOBAL COOPERATION FOR FOOD SECURITY

Many efforts are already under way to ensure long-term food security and prevent shortages. Scientists, aid organizations, and countries throughout the globe are working both independently and collaboratively to develop new food-production methods and to find more efficient means of transporting and distributing affordable food. Collaborative efforts in particular will prove vital in a global market. Certainly, considering that millions of people go hungry every day, these efforts are still far from solving the problem—but many agree that they may succeed in preventing a more serious food-supply collapse, at the same time slowly working to eradicate hunger.

SELF-RELIANCE AS FOOD AID

A major focus now is helping farmers in developing nations become more productive and, therefore, more self-reliant. Many poor farmers produce barely enough to support themselves, much less sell on the open market. In 2006, the Rockefeller and Bill and Melinda Gates foundations teamed up to invest in third-world agriculture in a project called the Alliance for a Green Revolution in Africa (AGRA). About seven in ten

Above: Global efforts by organizations such as the World Food Program (WFP) seek to pool resources on an international scale to fight hunger. Here, a Kenyan farmer (*right*) speaks with a WFP representative.

Africans make their living off agriculture, so the foundations directed hundreds of millions of dollars to aid native researchers, help replenish African soils, and provide fertilizer vouchers for farmers. A decade later, then-president of the Rockefeller Foundation Judith Rodin reported:

> Today, millions of farmers are using technologies that double their yields, moving from subsistence to profitability. Meanwhile, through support for higher education and other training, we have a new generation of agricultural leaders, whose work is already felt through new seeds, better markets, and private sector investments.

Still, there was more work to be done, and the Rockfeller Foundation committed an additional $50 million to support efforts to fight the impact of global warming and to double the income of thirty million households by 2020.

In a related plan, the Bill and Melinda Gates Foundation and others helped farmers grow food that they could then sell as food aid to the World Food Programme. In the past, most aid has been sent from far away, donated, or sold by developed nations. Foreign food aid often depresses prices for farmers in developing nations. Aid policies like those of the United States—which insists that its food aid be grown by its farmers and sent by American ships—have been criticized for adding billions in unnecessary costs. The new approach, a five-year pilot project called Purchase for Progress, helped an estimated 350,000 small farmers across twenty-one nations.

PRESERVING GENETIC DIVERSITY

About 700 miles (1,126 kilometers) south of the North Pole, in the Svalbard Islands of Norway, is perhaps the most unique of the seventeen hundred gene banks around the world that keep food-crop collections safe in case of catastrophe. In February 2008, the Svalbard Global Seed Vault was opened with the aim of preserving millions of different types of seeds for future use. Hidden deep within a mountainside, the vault now contains nearly nine hundred thousand samples—the most diverse variety in the world. The location of the vault ensures they will stay frozen even without power. When full, it is expected to hold about 2.5 billion seeds.

The Svalbard Islands in Norway are home to the Svalbard Global Seed Vault, where billions of seeds will eventually be stored for safekeeping.

The vault was established by the Global Crop Diversity Trust (GCDT), in part to protect the wide diversity of the planet's food, earning it the nickname the "Doomsday Seed Vault." The GCDT receives samples from international gene banks and uses scientists from around the world as "seed hunters" who go into remote places looking for important or rare varieties of crops.

The vault also helps preserve gene diversity, which scientists worry is a growing problem. Crops and other organisms need diverse gene pools to protect against disease, environmental change, and other threats. *Popular Science* reported in April 2008 that 75 percent of the variety within crops had disappeared in the last two centuries.

As then-direct of the GCDT Cary Fowler told the BBC, "Crop diversity will soon prove to be our most potent and indispensable resource for addressing climate change, water and energy constraints, and for meeting the food needs of a growing population." If any particular variety of crop were threatened, the vault could serve as a last resort to save it.

COMMERCIAL AGRICULTURE

In Brazil, different models of agriculture exist side by side. Many villagers farm using traditional techniques passed down for generations. In other areas, technology drives large, ultraprofitable agricultural companies. Some companies are so efficient that thirty minutes after a crop is harvested, another crop is planted in its place. In some cases, small, independent farmers working under a "contract farming" model provide a central company with their crops.

Economist Paul Collier, writing for *Foreign Affairs*, has argued that the Brazilian model would work for developing nations. "The world needs more commercial agriculture, not less," he wrote. "The Brazilian model of

Sustainable Farms

Sustainable farming methods are considered by many to be key to maintaining the health of the planet while fighting back against hunger and malnutrition.

With the rise of the organic foods industry and the environmentally conscious consumer, more small farmers are tackling the problems of energy and resources head-on. Phil Foster, an organic farmer in California, operates most of his tractors and trucks on biodiesel. He also uses renewable solar energy to help power his office, refrigerators, irrigation pumps, and other equipment.

For Foster, the move makes economic sense and appeals to customers. As he told *AlterNet* in 2006, "It was kind of a no-brainer for me to move in that direction. Especially in a business like ours, customers that buy organic would tend to like their growers to be kind of on the forefront." A decade later, Phil Foster Ranches continues to use these methods. It also works to attract helpful insects and owls so as to minimize the use of pest-control sprays.

high-productivity large farms could be readily extended to areas where land is underused." He dismissed organic, traditional agricultural as a romantic, unrealistic idea. "Far from being the answer to global poverty, organic self-sufficiency is a luxury lifestyle," he writes.

However, food writer and organic-foods advocate Michael Pollan, in an article for the *New York Times*, insisted that traditional methods do work. He used the example of Argentina, Brazil's neighbor. Farmers let cattle graze on pastures for five years, then grow grains on the same land for three years. Natural processes during both periods make artificial fertilizers and herbicides unnecessary. Pollan and others argue that such methods are better for the land and result in healthier food, and that future resource shortages make it crucial that countries like the United States invest in these techniques.

GMOS TO THE RESCUE?

Genetically modified foods have encountered a great deal of resistance in the United States. Increasing numbers of scientists and farmers, however, think that GM foods could help with food-supply problems and be environmentally safe. "To meet the appetites of the world's population without drastically hurting the environment requires a visionary new approach: combining genetic engineering and organic farming," wrote Pamela Ronald, a leading plant scientist with the University of California at Davis, in the *Boston Globe*.

GM crops that are resistant to flooding, drought, heat, and cold would help millions who farm in difficult environments, Ronald pointed out. Crops could also be bred to resist disease and pests, which can hurt farm productivity by 20 to 40 percent. The fact that many use less pesticide, which organic farmers favor, could be a big selling point.

Organic-friendly measures like crop rotation and beneficial insects could also be used with GM crops.

WHAT YOU CAN DO

While scientists and governments are busy planning for the future, there are ways that you can help. Maintaining an environmentally friendly diet could be the simplest way. Eating more vegetables and less meat helps save water, land, and energy, because raising livestock uses so much more of these resources. You can also look at ways to change your behavior to ensure you conserve energy, water, or even food (and save money, while you're at it). Taking shorter showers, turning off the lights when you leave the room, and making sure to eat leftovers are just a few places to start.

Supporting local food is another option. Food activists in cities

Employees at CEAGESP, home to Latin America's largest supply of vegetables and fruits, sort through a crate of tomatoes.

Young participants in Biscayne Bay Cleanup Day in Florida work with a solar-powered oven.

such as New York are promoting community-supported agriculture (CSA) programs to support the production of locally grown food. Sign up for a CSA to receive local produce on a regular basis. Empty plots of land in or near cities, whether public or private, are a huge potential resource for providing nutritious food while cutting the environmental costs of long-distance transportation, and many cities are transforming these areas into shared urban gardens.

Whether you favor organic or other solutions, there are many organizations you can find online or in your community that can provide information on how to help. Many of these need volunteers, too. If you cannot find an organization you like, or if you feel you have better ideas, start one yourself. By using the internet or asking around in your community or school, you can find like-minded people who care about change.

Food security may seem like an international issue, too large for any one person to make a difference—but the choices you make can have an enormous impact. Fighting food shortages is a collective effort, and raising awareness on the local level can decrease the use of fossil fuels for food transportation, encourage responsible land usage, and reduce food and water waste. Consider what you can do today, and every day, to make a difference.

GLOSSARY

agribusiness Agriculture performed on a large scale with industrial techniques.

arable Suitable for growing crops.

biofuel An alternative to gasoline produced from crops.

biotechnology The use of living organisms or biological tools to produce something.

casualty A person who has been injured or died.

crop rotation A system of farming in which different crops are grown on the same land during different growing seasons.

desalinization The process of removing salt from seawater to make freshwater for drinking and other uses.

drought An extended dry period or period without rain.

erosion The wearing-away of soil affected by wind, water, or ice.

famine An extended period of hunger leading to death and disease.

food security The reliable access to nutritious food.

food supply The total amount of food available to the world or to a particular nation or region.

gene bank A storage place for important seeds or crops.

global warming A rise in average world temperature caused mainly by human activities.

GMOs Genetically modified organisms; generally refers to crops or other organisms that have their genes changed to improve or enhance certain characteristics.

groundwater Water held underground in soil and rock.

herbicide A chemical used to control or kill weeds that interfere with or destroy crops.

mitigate To make less harmful or harsh.

organic Refers to farm products and farming methods in which artificial pesticides, herbicides, and fertilizers are avoided in favor of more natural alternatives.

petrochemicals Substances made from oil or natural gas.

self-sufficiency The ability of nations to provide their citizens with enough food without buying or importing it from elsewhere.

strain A type or variety of something, such as a crop or virus.

synthetic Something made artificially through chemical processes, often made to resemble a natural product.

voucher A document or receipt that can be used in place of cash to purchase something.

yield The amount of a crop produced or harvest.

FURTHER INFORMATION

BOOKS

Gay, Kathlyn. *Food: The New Gold*. Minneapolis, MN: Twenty-First Century Books, 2013.

Heinberg, Richard, and David Fridley. *Our Renewable Future: Laying the Path for One Hundred Percent Clean Energy*. Washington, DC: Island Press, Post Carbon Institute, 2016.

Liberti, Stefano. *Land Grabbing: Journeys in the New Colonialism*. Translated by Enda Flannelly. London and Brooklyn, NY: Verso, 2013.

Patel, Raj. *Stuffed and Starved: The Hidden Battle for the World Food System*. Brooklyn, NY: 2012.

WEBSITES

Food and Agriculture Organization of the United Nations

http://www.fao.org
The FAO publishes country profiles, statistics, and reports on food, agriculture, and hunger around the world.

International Fund for Agricultural Development

https://www.ifad.org
IFAD, a United Nations agency, works to improve the food security, nutrition, and income of people living in rural areas around the globe.

World Food Programme

http://www1.wfp.org
The World Food Programme helps eighty million people each year to improve nutrition and deliver food in emergencies. It publishes a report on food crises around the globe and other useful information about food shortages and hunger.

VIDEOS

A Global Food Crisis May Be Less Than a Decade Away

https://www.youtube.com/watch?v=OzA6jRYjVQs
In this 2017 video, Sara Menker—a data analyst and CEO/founder of Gro Intelligence, a company dedicated to increasing agricultural productivity—explains why the world may see a food crisis by 2027.

Food Insecurity: How It Happens and What You Can Do

https://www.youtube.com/watch?v=79UGlB1IRh4
This explanatory video from the British Red Cross explains the causes of food insecurity and how this can contribute to a cycle of hunger and poverty.

Global Report on Food Crises 2018

https://www.youtube.com/watch?v=0z8ORd1Icpo
The Food and Agriculture Organization of the United Nations offers an update on food insecurity around the world around the world.

ORGANIZATIONS

CARE

151 Ellis Street, NE
Atlanta, GA 30303
(800) 521-2273
http://www.care.org
CARE is a leading international humanitarian agency working in ninety-four countries to fight poverty, with an emphasis on women and families.

Centre for Studies in Food Security

Ryerson University
Kerr Hall South, 348 C
350 Victoria St
Toronto, ON M5B 0A1
(416) 979-5000 ext. 4538
http://www.ryerson.ca/foodsecurity
CSFS is an academic center at Ryerson University engaging in research, education, and community action on food security issues.

Food Secure Canada

3875 St-Urbain, Suite 502
Montreal, QC H2W 1V1
(514) 271-7352
http://www.acdi-cida.gc.ca/index-e.htm
This alliance of people and organizations throughout Canada
seeks to promote sustainable food systems and safe, healthy food
throughout the country with the goal of ending hunger.

Oxfam America

226 Causeway Street, 5th Floor
Boston, MA 02114
(800) 776-9326
http://www.oxfamamerica.org
Oxfam America is the US branch of an international nonprofit
organization dedicated to fighting poverty and promoting social
justice.

US Agency for International Development

Ronald Reagan Building
Washington, DC 20523-1000
(202) 712-0000
http://www.usaid.gov
USAID is the leading government-based organization providing
foreign nations in need with economic development and disaster
relief, including antihunger campaigns.

US Department of Agriculture

1400 Independence Avenue SW
Washington, DC 20250
http://www.usda.gov
The USDA is the US government agency responsible for policies
on food and agriculture.

BIBLIOGRAPHY

"About Phil Foster Ranches." Pinnacle Organically Grown Produce. Accessed May 6, 2018. http://www.pinnacleorganic.com/AboutOurFarm.html.

Aderibigbe, Niyi. "How Bill Gates Plans to Help Africa Feed Itself." *Ventures Africa*, January 27, 2015. http://venturesafrica.com/how-bill-gates-plans-to-help-africa-feed-itself.

Arsenault, Chris. "Risk of Water Wars Rises with Scarcity." Al Jazeera, August 26, 2012. https://www.aljazeera.com/indepth/features/2011/06/2011622193147231653.html.

Barbet-Gros, Julie, and Jose Cuesta. "Food Riots: From Definition to Operationalization." World Bank. Accessed May 6, 2018. http://www.worldbank.org/content/dam/Worldbank/document/Poverty%20documents/Introduction%20Guide%20for%20the%20Food%20Riot%20Radar.pdf.

Cambanis, Thanassis. "The Arab Spring Was a Revolution of the Hungry." *Boston Globe*, August 23, 2015. https://www.bostonglobe.com/ideas/2015/08/22/the-arab-spring-was-revolution-hungry/K15S1kGeO5Y6gsJwAYHejI/story.html.

"Committee on World Food Security." Food and Agriculture Organization of the United Nations, 2015. http://www.fao.org/3/a-au831e.pdf.

Donnelly, Jim. "The Irish Famine." BBC, February 17, 2011. http://www.bbc.co.uk/history/british/victorians/famine_01.shtml.

"EU Actions Against Food Waste." European Commission, May 7, 2018. https://ec.europa.eu/food/safety/food_waste/eu_actions_en.

Figueroa, Melania, and Peter Dodds. "Breakthrough in the Battle against Ug99." Borlaug Global Rust Initiative, January 25, 2018. https://www.globalrust.org/blog/breakthrough-battle-against-ug99.

"Food Price Watch, June 2015: Prices Hit Five-Year Low; Impact of Low Oil Price on Global Food Prices, Poverty and Inequality." World Bank, 2015. http://www.worldbank.org/en/topic/poverty/publication/food-price-watch-june-2015-prices-hit-five-year-low-impact-of-low-oil-price-on-global-food-prices-poverty-and-inequality.

"Genetically Modified (GM) Rice." International Rice Research Institute. Accessed May 6, 2018. http://irri.org/news/hot-topics/genetically-modified-gm-rice.

Gray, Richard. "How Can We Manage Earth's Land?" BBC, June 29, 2017. http://www.bbc.com/future/story/20170628-how-to-best-manage-earths-land.

Harris, Paul. "Monsanto Sued Small Farmers to Protect Seed Patents, Report Says." *Guardian* (UK), February 12, 2013. https://www.theguardian.com/environment/2013/feb/12/monsanto-sues-farmers-seed-patents.

Kay, Jane. "Overfishing Imperils Ocean Life, Study Says." *San Francisco Chronicle*, March 3, 2009. http://www.sfgate.com/cgi-bin/article.cgi?f=/c/a/2009/03/03/BAGQ167VF6.DTL.

Khokhar, Tariq. "Chart: Globally, 70% of Freshwater Is Used for Agriculture." World Bank, Data Blog, March 22, 2017. https://blogs.worldbank.org/opendata/chart-globally-70-freshwater-used-agriculture.

Kirby, Alex. "Dawn of a Thirsty Century." BBC News, June 2, 2000. http://news.bbc.co.uk/2/hi/science/nature/755497.stm.

Kluger, Jeffrey. "The Suicide Seeds." *Time*, February 1, 1999. http://www.time.com/time/magazine/article/0,9171,990111,00.html.

Landry, Heather. "Challenging Evolution: How GMOs Can Influence Genetic Diversity." *Science in the News*, Harvard University, Graduate School of Arts and Sciences, August 10, 2015. http://sitn.hms.harvard.edu/flash/2015/challenging-evolution-how-gmos-can-influence-genetic-diversity.

Lavelle, Marianne, and Kent Garber. "8 Ways to Fix the Global Food Crisis." *U.S. News & World Report*, May 9, 2008. http://www.usnews.com/articles/news/2008/05/09/8-ways-to-fix-the-global-food-crisis.html.

Lohan, Tara. "A World Without Water." *Nation*, February 16, 2009. http://www.thenation.com/doc/20090302/lohan?rel=hp_currently.

Mackenzie, Debora. "Billions at Risk from Wheat Super-blight." *New Scientist*, April 2007. http://www.newscientist.com/article/mg19425983.700-billions-at-risk-from-wheat-superblight.html.

Mark, Jason. "Will the End of Oil Be the End of Food?" *AlterNet*, August 31, 2006. http://www.alternet.org/story/41023.

McWilliams, James E. "Could Frankenfoods Be Good for the Environment?" *Slate*, January 28, 2009. http://www.slate.com/id/2209168.

Milman, Oliver. "Earth Has Lost a Third of Arable Land in past 40 Years, Scientists Say." *Guardian* (UK), December 2, 2015. https://www.theguardian.com/environment/2015/dec/02/arable-land-soil-food-security-shortage.

Milman, Oliver, and Stuart Leavenworth. "China's Plan to Cut Meat Consumption by 50% Cheered by Climate Campaigners." *Guardian* (UK), June 20, 2016. https://www.theguardian.com/world/2016/jun/20/chinas-meat-consumption-climate-change.

"More Seeds for 'Doomsday Vault.'" BBC News, February 26, 2009. http://news.bbc.co.uk/1/hi/sci/tech/7912543.stm.

Newman, Brian. "Companies Can Help Solve Water Scarcity. Here's How." World Economic Forum, March 15, 2018. https://www.weforum.org/agenda/2018/03/companies-can-help-solve-water-scarcity-here-s-how.

Nichols, John. "The World Food Crisis." *Nation*, May 12, 2008. http://www.thenation.com/doc/20080512/nichols.

Parker, Laura. "What You Need to Know About the World's Water Wars." *National Geographic*, July 14, 2016. https://news.nationalgeographic.com/2016/07/world-aquifers-water-wars.

"Plant Pests and Diseases." Food and Agriculture Organization of the United Nations, FAO in Emergencies. Accessed May 6, 2018. http://www.fao.org/emergencies/emergency-types/plant-pests-and-diseases/en.

Pollan, Michael. "Farmer in Chief." *New York Times Magazine*, October 9, 2008. http://www.nytimes.com/2008/10/12/magazine/12policy-t.html.

"President Resigns After Riots Leave 22 Dead in Argentina." *Daily Mail* (UK), December 28, 2012. http://www.dailymail.co.uk/news/article-91169/President-resigns-riots-leave-22-dead-Argentina.html.

Reuters. "'They're Hunting. The People Are Hungry!' Venezuelans Are Rioting Over Food Shortages." *Fortune*, January 12, 2018. http://fortune.com/2018/01/11/venezuela-food-riots.

Roberts, Paul. "Food Fight." *Slate*, August 8, 2008. http://www.slate.com/id/2196772.

Rodin, Judith. "Agriculture is the Engine of Growth that Africa Needs." Rockefeller Foundation, September 7, 2016. https://www.rockefellerfoundation.org/blog/agriculture-engine-growth-africa-needs.

Rogers, Peter. "Facing the Freshwater Crisis." *Scientific American*, July 2008. http://www.sciam.com/article.cfm?id=facing-the-freshwater-crisis.

Ronald, Pamela. "The New Organic." *Boston Globe*, March 16, 2008. http://www.boston.com/bostonglobe/ideas/articles/2008/03/16/the_new_organic.

Rosner, Hillary. "Seeds to Save a Species." *Popular Science*, April 2008. http://www.popsci.com/scitech/article/2008-01/seeds-save-species.

Spector, Dina. "Here's How Many Days a Person Can Survive Without Water." *Business Insider*, March 8, 2018. http://www.businessinsider.com/how-many-days-can-you-survive-without-water-2014-5.

"Stop Food Waste." European Commission, May 6, 2018. https://ec.europa.eu/food/safety/food_waste/eu_actions_en.

"Svalbard Global Seed Vault." Crop Trust. Accessed May 6, 2018. https://www.croptrust.org/our-work/svalbard-global-seed-vault.

"2016 Crop Year Report." California Department of Food and Agriculture. Accessed May 6, 2018. https://www.cdfa.ca.gov/statistics.

van Dijk, Albert I. J. M., Hylke E. Beck, Russell S. Crosbie, Richard A. M. de Jeu, Yi Y. Liu, Geoff M. Podger, Bertrand Timbal, and Neil R. Viney. "The Millennium Drought in Southeast Australia (2001–2009): Natural and Human Causes and Implications for Water Resources, Ecosystems, Economy, and Society." *Water Resources Research* 49 (February 6, 2013). https://agupubs.onlinelibrary.wiley.com/doi/full/10.1002/wrcr.20123.

Walt, Vivienne. "The World's Growing Food-Price Crisis." *Time*, February 27, 2008. http://www.time.com/time/world/article/0,8599,1717572,00.html.

Wehrfritz, George. "Shortages Are on the Horizon." *Newsweek*, February 27, 2008. http://www.newsweek.com/id/116649.

"World Population Prospects: The 2017 Revision." United Nations, Department of Economic and Social Affairs, June 21, 2017. https://www.un.org/development/desa/publications/world-population-prospects-the-2017-revision.html.

INDEX

Page numbers in **boldface** are illustrations.

ABOUT THE AUTHOR

Erin L. McCoy is a literature, language, and cultural studies educator and an award-winning photojournalist and poet. She holds a master of arts degree in Hispanic studies and a master of fine arts in creative writing from the University of Washington. She has edited nearly twenty nonfiction books for young adults, including *The Mexican-American War* and *The Israel-Palestine Border Conflict* from the Redrawing the Map series with Cavendish Square Publishing. She is from Louisville, Kentucky.